# The Weather in Normal

*for Trevor*

# The Weather in Normal
*Carrie Etter*

Seren is the book imprint of
Poetry Wales Press Ltd.
57 Nolton Street, Bridgend, Wales, CF31 3AE
www.serenbooks.com
facebook.com/SerenBooks
twitter@SerenBooks

ISBN: 978-1-78172-459-0
ebook: 978-1-78172-460-6
Kindle: 978-1-78172-461-3

A CIP record for this title is available from the British Library.

The publisher acknowledges the financial assistance of the Welsh Books Council.

Cover photograph: 'Thunderstorm Lightning – Central Illinois'
by Jason P. Ross.

Printed in Bembo by Bell & Bain Ltd, Glasgow.

# Contents

*The gods wait in the corn.*

– Sherwood Anderson, "Song of the Lonely Roads"


*And there goes our little world, set upon its haunches,*
*fraught with neglect –*

– Safiya Sinclair, "I Shall Account Myself a Happy Creaturess"

I

# Night Ode

Hovey Avenue, coursed by vehicles day into night,
goes quiet at last.

No, not quiet, not with the cicadas squalling in the trees,
and yet.

At midnight, I emerge from the shadowed sidewalk to tread
the street's center line.

The third hundred-plus day in a row, everyone's abed
or torpid before

television screens when I float past on the night's first
cool breath.

I walk the length and no cars, people, dogs – just me, sixteen,
nineteen, twenty-four,

thirty-seven … the night my horse, my brimful wine,
my very own.

# Fatherhood

The weather belongs to everyone, so you may say, but in our family, it was his. It was his study by internet, television, radio, barometer, and long rides cycling past the cornfields in all their seasons and moods. He witnessed and reported, and when I moved away, he expanded his research accordingly, learned my temperature, precipitation, wind speed, and humidity. He marveled at my extremes – the Northridge earthquake, a tornado in London. By phone he told me my weather, and sometimes I listened. Sometimes I spoke of the sun and the rain as though I held one in either hand.

# My Father and the Blizzard

*All italicized passages come from M.K. Guetersloh and Mary Ann Ford's article,
"Blizzard brings central Illinois to a snow halt,"* The Pantagraph, *14 February 2007.*

as the snow fell    the man's pain surged    three short shrieks, staccato
his wife sat bedside    as a nurse bestowed morphine

       all windows gone white

*The large storm moved into the Twin Cities late Monday night, and snow began to
fall just after midnight.*

the doctor phoned in    snow rising in drifts    around his house

    he asked the nurse
                    "Is it life-threatening?"

*By Tuesday morning, nearly 4 inches had fallen and schools and businesses closed
for the day.*

and so the morphine until    the man stopped breathing

*By late afternoon, 10.5 inches of snow had fallen at Normal, according to the
National Weather Service.*

a ventilator restored his breath but

*Primary streets in Bloomington and Normal were nearly the only roads open as plow
crews had trouble keeping up with the falling and blowing snow.*

at last the doctor    and the man, now in intensive care

    *whiteout conditions*       *drifting snow*

coma    a weatherless world

# Eldest

Lean forward in shadow. The room is corridor opening into square, passage and purpose.

On the distant bed, a spill of mottled flesh, the white cotton gown fallen to little use. You gape in the doorway. His body is positioned away, toward the window. You stare until he calls, calls you into mutual shame.

Now you must gentle. The mind, relieved, packs away its unfinished question. The bowl of green gelatin has no scent. You hold it to your nose as he draws the cloth up with a tug, his grasp like a bird's.

No, not shame. Not now. Though he doesn't know it, he will be glad when you sit down at last. This is your father. The room is white and inescapable.

## Those Winters

The cornfields now milk-brown stubble,
the wind has more range to rip and howl.

In town it clatters the glass; it refuses and cries
like a missing bear cub
or, rather, its mother.

★

My mother fell and she broke
She despised the cold on her face, in her joints
She slid
She could've explained black ice, the inherent contradiction
She slid, she fell, she broke
She was unbreakable
She had arms twenty, thirty feet wide, a wingspan
She had a wingspan not visible to the naked eye
She broke a few times figuratively and literally once
She fell on the ice
She slid and took her weight on her hand and her wrist and crack
She who wrote who taught who mothered on the right hand
She fell and she fell and she fell and none of us
Unbreakable, I said, she was unbreakable

★

The second Christmas after the father's layoff,
the mother suggested to her girls
the usual, small things: socks     chocolate     a book
        and one something-larger each

The eldest, fifteen, asked to spend it in thrift shops

One frozen day, on Mulberry Street, she walked in,
and a cragged, beaming woman said *today*     *today*
        *all you can fit in a bag for a dollar*

on this rack, a slightly musty, red wool coat
on this, a button-down shirt     her father's size and color
here, a Steinbeck novel     here, a black cardigan

Christmas morning, behind the twinkling tree, five bulging

brown paper bags

★

She who blamed the annual freeze
for arthritic aches, for the pain
in knees and knuckles,

who placed before him the word: *Arizona*:

(how it shone!)

she joined *Arizona* with *please*,
and I hear his silence
long after their deaths.

★

And of the "Valentine's Day Blizzard" of 2007
with a father, in the hospital for a kidney biopsy, shrieking?
And of the doctor who – given the storm –
asked the nurse if it was life-threatening?
And the shrieking man who,
amid the blizzard, stopped breathing?
And who, waking weeks later,
could not lift his limbs?

Winter, I tell you. Fucking winter.

# Song a Year after My Mother's Death

I allowed a small song
to nestle between my breasts.
It was furtive, a ground squirrel
occasionally checking the wind.

I thought it could not grow
on wine and despair. It didn't.
On the one sunny day in a rainy month,
it basked.

It took on color: peacock blue
shimmering like sunlit sea. I feared
it would strut. I watched
it fly forth

afraid of no one, no one
but me.

# Artifact

*All italicized passages come from Roddy Lumsden's poem, "The World."*

Dad's Kennedy and Stevenson buttons, my mother's many cards signed with Xs and Os, photographs from cameras become obsolete, the occasional, momentous ticket stub, *the gone restored in niches,* but restored for whom? I want the immortality of what I prize, *a pure song snug in the head.* There's no downloading such elaborate intricacy, *distilled to a tot,* oh no. Oh no.

\*

*A key in the palm of the hand,* a poem, a hand-thrown vase. I want *animal precision,* I want *dark reason skittled.* O my archeologist, take your fine brush, pick away a little dust, turn this twice in your hands.

II

# Prairie

Illinois, below Chicago and its suburbs       the flatness

beginning with the Latin *partum*       meadow, a word that for me

always evoked an idyll       eclogue       Arcadia

on to the old French *praerie*       a matter of scale

from meadow to       North America       the boundaries

blown wide       so in the late eighteenth century       *prairie*

*level or slightly undulating       mostly treeless tract*

so Illinoisans were never raised       for hills

*prairie*       the horizon the very       edge of the world

# Trying to Say

Sometimes I explain home        as a list:
a cardinal's flash of red        against snow
the prairie's flatness      green stalks rising
a milkweed pod      its fit in the palm
        fat and taut with tufted seeds

Sometimes I explain home      by the way I speak
a surely brightening face    and the most banal
recollections          urgently offered

Sometimes I explain home          by drawing out the syllables
        *Ill*         *lih*          *noy*
and reclining        in the breadth        the breath of it

# Afterlife

You're back                                    & tremble
on the sidewalk beside                    childhood
beside                                the house / home


can I put merely before              imagination
you're merely there                in imagination
& yet                                              tremble


and the scent:              poplars

                                                        after rain

consider                    the absences outside:
the peeling                 pop-up camper the
wooden picnic table              & those poplars


& him &                                    & her

consider                              inside:
a long succession         of felines, often tabbies
and those five                   Etter girls then

their children                 streaming through
(once three sat atop        the upright piano
playing the keys                 with their feet)

and from the kitchen:              her lasagna
peanut brittle       and on New Year's Eve, home-
made Chex mix                savory, hot & salty

(him &                                       her)

consider the absences

before

And so out of                                    the house
and no farther


                                                 the front step
whether concrete or wood              marks its time

the concrete until                                his paralysis
then a wooden patio              becoming a long ramp

built by volunteers

there                                            one long summer
his skin gone brown                     as he gazed west

```
gazing west                          the prairie sunset
all the sky                                        in it

blurring bands, streaks: fuchsia, yellow, lilac
blue above not so much boundary as


                                    rupture
```

before or behind                                  a screen door
its black mesh                           not become invisible
yet unseen

                        so what's viewed seems unobstructed
unmediated
                                                    whole

despite the black grid the

door                                              before the door

and so you find yourself                              within
you thought you had                                emerged?

from the age of five                           which could be
the age of memory                                this house

and the tree out front                          then a sapling
now mature its                                  canopy shading

                                           where everyone slept

goldenrod                      long before you saw the plant
a shade of paint                  covering the house

           g o l d e n r o d

                    the word *brimmed*

gave the house                      a poetry

before you knew what

turning back                                              to the living room
in December                                        the scent of pine, the tree
in the chill                                  from the large front window

smudged again and again                                         with faces
to gaze on                                                        arrivals

who is it                                               pulling into the drive
who walks                                                       up the path

the glass and all                                      those unwitting kisses

upstairs                              the bedrooms
downstairs                              including

the crawl space                    under the house
a world of                      mice & spiders & cats
you refused                             to risk it


may have been                      the house's core
the absence holding up          so much presence

& her                                              suffuses

every room
presence                                    in abrupt traces

foremost
her collection of                              lighthouses

wood, plastic, ceramic              strewn through


                                                  a landlocked life

so you loiter                    in the living room
                                      here he died

                                 you watched him die

do you wait                           for his ghost?

but you
you whisper the candle-flame

                              flicker, gutter, gone

to live
at this junction                              breath & memory
                                            shifting proportions

his body on a hospice bed
now a sofa

what ghosts are here

                    but you?

so leave as a familiar might          out the back
open the glass door                   into twilight
& walk toward the absent                  poplars

as sliding doors lock             only from within
you needn't                          pause or turn
when the new residents'            talk bubbles up

and lights
                  in this room, that

                                           blaze

III

# An Invocation

*for beginning to write about climate change*

If eloquence were flour and anger were yeast
that I knead hour upon hour,

and the sprinkle of salt's either
my tears or my spit,

I'd watch the dough rise
before I punch it back down,

feel my fists become fingers,
fingers become fists

# Karner Blue

*"...a place called Karner, where in some pine barrens, on lupines,*
*a little blue butterfly I have described and named ought to be out."*
            —Vladimir Nabokov


Because it used to be more populous in Illinois.
Because its wingspan is an inch.
Because it requires blue lupine.
Because to become blue, it has to ingest the leaves of a blue plant.
Because its scientific name, *Lycaeides melissa samuelis*, is mellifluous.
Because the female is not only blue but blue and orange and silver and black.
Because its beauty galvanizes collectors.
Because Nabokov named it.
Because its collection is criminal.
Because it lives in black oak savannahs and pine barrens.
Because it once produced landlocked seas.
Because it has declined ninety per cent in fifteen years.
Because it is.

# Parable

The water in the boat's hold is five feet high, and I have a thimble for the bailing. Each day the duty roster remains the same: I take the burden longer than any member of my crew. Weeks pass with no appreciable progress, and at least daily the tiny steel cup slips from my fingers, to be rescued from the murk after lost minutes, sometimes an hour. After months, we find a shipwreck survivor on a dinghy, and in gratitude he offers me his bucket. I throw it into the sea to show him the magnitude of my work.

# Scar

*i.m. Peter Reading*

at my beginning:       prairie

at my beginning:             a town called       Normal


      on the far horizon                cornfield upon cornfield splayed

                     flattened by tornado


              stunted stalks, palest soil under      a heavy sun

            soybeans       submerged in water

but no –      not far:


            today, tomorrow

so here's     The White House's "Fact Sheet:
                What Climate Change Means

                                  for Illinois and the Midwest"

its list, its gist

      the volume's rising:

              more heat
              more pests
              more disease

              more extreme weather events:

                        tornado
                        drought
                        flood
                        heat wave
                        blizzard

O Illinois –

more tornadoes

      one scours a half-mile-wide path through Fairdale

      flattens / twists / hurls      homes / cars / a child's treehouse

      its scar in the earth visible

                from space

(off-page I am

      feline slink,

            butterfly shiver,

                  fish glide, I am

                        animal amid)

more tornadoes

    and if you haven't a basement or cellar?

                                who hasn't a basement or cellar?

    apartment-, trailer-home dwellers


      yeah, you know

more heat waves

and in Chicago, amid concrete, asphalt          heat islands

    *heat islands*


    and who lives there?

(In Illinois, am I the cicada
    gnawing through summer nights,


the cow raising its gaze
    at the wind's shift,


the field mouse scrabbling
    in grain-rich dirt...)

more droughts

in Illinois, a farmer crumbles
earth between thumb and forefinger

and in Egypt, a mother counts coins, reckons
the cost of bread

more floods

and the crops drown      go to mud

"A year's amount of rain in a month
and a half: 25 to 30 inches of rain," one farmer said.


"It's a wonder we aren't all alcoholics."

(into air I become the awe of red or yellow

    cardinal or goldfinch and

at times more modest

    house wren or sparrow

not even a quiver

    along the branch)

more blizzards

the descent quickens     thickens
less and less sky     tree     land
more and more white and the wind
a low whistle speeds into a whine
a quake in the panes
and now only an occasional flicker of color
amid the white throttling          the house

In the kitchen, the buzz of the CB radio.
He raises the microphone to his mouth:
*Break 31 for Cindy Bear –*
*Cindy Bear, are you there?*

I – nine? ten? – stand in the dining room's peripheral darkness
and watch him flick dials,
switch between the emergency channel
and our usual and back again.
My father grows smaller –
can one *grow* – yes, he grows – smaller,
he sweats, he calls again, he begs,
he says *she was going to Zayre's*, he says

(he doesn't say *hey hey hey this is Yogi Bear!*)

white shakes the glass and I realize
I'm holding my breath –

along the Mackinaw

                 plant trees and more trees

      to shade, to cool

                    smallmouth bass

                          southern redbelly, blacknose dace

and head northwest     to the sand prairies

      make them safe            and the ornate box turtle    thrives

now to find rocky outcrops    nurture oak openings

     for the slender glass lizard     timber rattlesnakes

and last *(never last)*             and here *(and here, and here)*

      the wetlands:          common moorhens

         king rails          marsh wrens:

     so they live

*The apologies shine like coins in the bowels of a fountain –*

(and I burrow down

amid beetle and muskrat

woodchuck and snake

worm and rabbit

tunneling in the sure)

more tornadoes

sirens
       and the children *s t r e a m*

       away from glass

            into, huddle against

    face the hallway's brick walls
    all those         primary colors
    so many       balls of skin and bone

every month, the children practice
  shield their bodies against
                 the possible

*the apology song with its one shrill note —*

more blizzards

       snow and more snow until the roads
          are no longer roads

       and a helicopter – with such snow, such winds –
          cannot deliver the heart

                    in time

(it's true: I bark and coo, swim and wriggle
flutter and slide, snort and screech –

am animal amid animals –


and I annihilate.


I, the world's curse.)

# And Now for a Kind of Song

A strain of the common, cornstalk & flatland
of weather hot & wet to cold & dry
of cow, rabbit, squirrel & mouse
& cicada louder than all else
perhaps wordless, perhaps a mere handful of notes
hummed through fields, along sidewalks, on trails
a tune one murmurs in distraction, without thought
a song in the body, the body in Illinois

# *Acknowledgements*

Thanks to the editors of the following publications, where many poems in this collection first appeared: *A Change of Climate, Compass, Court Green, Handsome, New Letters, New Walk, Oxford Poetry, Plume, Poetry Ireland Review, Poetry Review,* and *The Rialto.* "Scar" was published as a chapbook (*Scar*) by Shearsman Books, and a section of the poem was published as "Conservation" in *women : migration : poetry [an anthology]* (Theenk Books).

For assistance with individual poems in the book, I am grateful to my workshop groups in London and Somerset, as well as individual poets Susie Campbell, Forrest Gander, Anna-May Laugher, Peter Riley, and Heidi Williamson. For their readings of the complete manuscript, I must thank Matt Bryden, Claire Crowther, Ian Duhig, and Zoë Brigley Thompson. Bath Spa University provided teaching relief in the 2015-16 academic year, which proved crucial for developing the work. Lastly, thanks to the many fellow poets, friends, and students who have given nourishing support and to my husband Trevor Lillistone for everything.

The poem "Scar" was informed by the following works: "Updating the Illinois Wildlife Action Plan: Using a vulnerability assessment to inform conservation priorities"; Naomi Klein's *This Changes Everything*; The White House's "Fact Sheet: What Climate Change Means for Illinois and the Midwest," dated 6 May 2014; the Environmental Justice Climate Change report, "Climate of Change: African-Americans, Global Warming and Just Climate Policy"; a day with former senior scientist Rachel McCarthy at The Met Office; and conversations and interviews with Illinoisans.

The passage from Safiya Sinclair's "I Shall Account Myself a Happy Creaturess" is reproduced from her collection *Cannibal* by permission of the University of Nebraska Press, copyright 2016 by the Board of Regents of the University of Nebraska; and the passages from Roddy Lumsden's "The World" from his collection *Terrific Melancholy* are reproduced by permission of Bloodaxe Books, copyright 2011.

# About the Author

Carrie Etter lived her first nineteen years in Normal, Illinois, before taking a one-way train to Los Angeles. While living in southern California, she founded and edited (and later co-edited) *Out Loud: The Monthly of Los Angeles Area Poetry Events* and pursued her BA in English at UCLA and MFA in creative writing and MA and PhD in English at the University of California, Irvine. She moved to England in 2001 and began teaching in 2004 at Bath Spa University, where she is a Reader in Creative Writing. She has published three previous collections of poems: *The Tethers* (Seren, 2009), winner of the London New Poetry Prize for the best first collection published in the UK and Ireland in the preceding year; *Divining for Starters* (Shearsman, 2011); and *Imagined Sons* (Seren, 2014), shortlisted for the Ted Hughes Award for New Work in Poetry by The Poetry Society. She also edited *Infinite Difference: Other Poetries by UK Women Poets* (Shearsman, 2010) and Linda Lamus's posthumous collection, *A Crater the Size of Calcutta* (Mulfran, 2015). Additionally she writes essays, short fiction, and reviews.